D1155451

A TENDER OF PEACE

A TENDER
OF PEACE

THE TERMS ON WHICH
CIVILIZED NATIONS
CAN, IF THEY WILL,
AVOID WARFARE

BY

JOHN BATES CLARK

MORNINGSIDE HEIGHTS

COLUMBIA UNIVERSITY PRESS

NEW YORK: MCMXXXV

Copyright 1935
COLUMBIA UNIVERSITY PRESS

Published 1935

PRINTED IN THE UNITED STATES OF AMERICA
THE PLIMPTON PRESS, NORWOOD, MASS.

ST. OLAF COLLEGE LIBRARY
NORTHFIELD, MINN.

CONTENTS

40733

A TENDER OF PEACE

can be averted is the evolution that created modern states and has recently brought them into more and more intimate relations. It has made them capable of reasoning together and taking common action for great ends. This is apparent if we glance in even the briefest way at certain historical facts and then at certain principles of human nature by which organized societies are controlled. The measure of peace that the modern world has enjoyed has been due, first to impulses in primitive man which led to state building, and, second, to tendencies in men of today that are capable of bringing the several states together in a harmonious community.

We are dwelling today on a wonderfully " shrunken " planet. Journeys that encircle the world are as common as once were those across straits or mountain ranges, and no nations are now so widely separated that they are not, in essential ways, dependent on one another. No one of them can maintain its present level of life and comfort without coöperating with others; and this means that there now exists an *economic community of free states,* having common interests and effective means of promoting them. They face, however, very critical problems, and every success in solving these problems registers an upward step in the general life of man. His present world-wide commonwealth is superior to anything that earlier centuries witnessed, but it has not yet progressed beyond the possibility of very serious danger. Shall there henceforth be permanent peace or the intermittent warfare with which all the ages have been familiar? Shall this warfare bring ruin that will greatly surpass former ruin, and shall a practice amounting to interstate massacre reappear? It is these questions that our generation has to decide. Although measures already taken have made strongly for peace and a life that will be worth living, there is one long step still untaken. If this step is soon taken, it should carry us beyond the zone of doubt and deadly peril in which we have heretofore lived. No cobweb structure is the existing League of Nations. It is much greater, more firmly united and more efficient than was any previous union of free peoples. What needs to be fully appreciated is the tendency toward general and friendly coöperation which has existed in small fields of action from early times but which is now acting in a world-wide field and with increasing effectiveness.

The old world cherished no hope of universal and enduring peace at any time short of the millennium. In lieu of such a hope for peace it established a " tolerance " of war, as men sometimes establish what in medical parlance is " tolerance " of a disease of which they cannot rid themselves. From immemorial times, the world has lived its life as best it could with the germs of intermittent warfare in its system. Does it still harbor those germs? Are we satisfied to eat and drink while we can, knowing that at some time not far in the future the war demons will have their way? It is both safe and delightful to be able to say that such is not the present mental attitude of the world. Peoples are growing less acquiescent in the continued prospect of chronic warfare; but an expectation of peace that will never hereafter be broken is not yet widely cherished. The world has outlying areas in which war still flourishes and may continue to flourish. Civil war is today a specialty in certain regions, the people of which have been obliged to order their lives as best they could, with warfare ever and anon claiming many of their young men and wrecking countless lives.

If most wars had been like the World War there would have been little now worth living for in any nation; and that there will be little worth living for, it is safe to say, will actually be the case hereafter, if wars are not prevented or very narrowly circumscribed. They can, however, be prevented. The route to peace is open, and nations can, if they so will, see it and walk therein. In various regions in which war has, at times, done its worst, there seems to be *a fair chance of putting it out of the range of probability for a long enough time to allow institutions to develop that should prevent it from ever reappearing.* We now dare to hope for the erstwhile impossible. If our action is on the moral level of our hope, this goal will be reached. In their relations with each other individual men have developed rules of conduct that are on an appreciably higher moral plane than were those of early times. Interstate relations are in an early stage of a similar evolution that will give, first on one continent and then on others, a conditional promise of ending warfare.

What are the conditions? How shall wars now be prevented? Between man and man in local communities the resources for peaceful living are laws and courts backed by armed forces that are too strong to be challenged. Can a system akin to this be established in an interstate community? Can armed aggressors be halted, as miscreants are halted, by armed policemen?

WAR AND ETHICS

THE earliest wars were both more savage and more morally innocent than any that have since been waged. They followed man's primitive struggle for survival and partook of its character. Tribes living on game and wild fruits were often hard pressed for food, and when two of them were dependent on land that afforded nourishment for only one, a fight for existence was inevitable — and it was a fight to the bitter end. Prisoners were slain because they could not safely be provided with weapons for hunting, lest they use them for slaying their captors. In the background of their early experience such tribes found little that taught the sacredness of life — especially the life of an enemy. Precepts on this subject were of later growth. When states whose moral codes are well developed initiate wars, very dark is the guilt thereof; and guilt would be at its darkest if now another world war were allowed to occur. That would be sinning on a vast scale, against the clearest light and in spite of adequate power of prevention. Another world war would concentrate in itself more stark iniquity than was perpetrated in centuries of fighting under the early conditions.

On the highest American authority " war is hell." That monosyllable stands for the extreme of both guilt and suffering, and it invites us to inquire against whom the moral indictment for it properly lies. Is it against soldiers who obey orders, or commanders who give orders, or statesmen who bring about the quarrels that later set armies in motion? Can the statesmen shift the responsibility to the people whose servants they are? Discrimination is assuredly necessary for tracing the " incidence " of the case against war. It is, moreover, clear that there are sins of omission as well as of commission to be taken into account. It is a capital crime not to prevent warfare when it can be prevented, and also not to try to prevent it when there is the slightest chance that the attempt can succeed.

Before trying to apportion blame among classes within a nation it is essential to make sure whether in wars as we know them moral condemnation is due alike to both contending parties; and fortunately this question admits of a self-evident answer. Fighting is a two-sided operation, but the chief guilt of it is usually on one side. There is, as we shall see, a chance for some exceptions to this rule, and in an earlier and ruder age there were such constant incentives to fighting that very few persons were as scrupulous concerning the moral implications as the majority of any civilized people now are. We are here speaking of the time in which we live and of nations that make war, whenever they do so, with a degree of regularity of procedure. Under such conditions there is a distinguishable aggressor in nearly every case, and we shall see why it is indispensable, in international dealings, to recognize this fact and act accordingly. If there is a difficulty in our way, we must overcome it.

A robber and his victim are not in the same class, though both may fight and both may even try to kill. Modern nations, as well as primitive tribes, have often stood ready to seize their neighbors' territories, and force of some kind has always been needed for thwarting such intentions. An attempted seizure and resistance by the victims constitute a war, and the defense has its share in the physical barbarities. If all shooting to kill is murder, then both of the contesting forces in any war descend into the pit together; but the universal verdict of the world does not fail to draw distinctions. Morally, war is a dual action. There are always two parties engaged in it, and, whenever there is an overt attack by one power and only a defense by the other, their moral positions are as unlike as darkness and light. If the offense calls for " deep damnation," the defense calls for unstinted praise — and seldom fails to get it. Tamely to surrender while a hope of successful defense remains would expose a people to general contempt. It is as wicked as it is disgraceful to shirk the duty of defending home and country.

It is difficult to state strongly enough the moral contrast between offensive and defensive warfare. Calling defense " excusable " would be grotesquely underrating its merits. It is infinitely more than excusable. At great sacrifice defenders do a sacred duty — one which is sanctioned by God and man — and they earn the plaudits that are always lavished on them. Leonidas, Arnold Winkelried, and a multitude of others like them are " with the immortals " in a special Valhalla reserved for those who die in a holy cause. The world owes them a debt of gratitude for the standard of heroism that they have set for men of every land and age. Emulation of their acts has enriched the world with a fund of latent heroism which ripens into deeds in times of national danger. The battlefield is certainly not, physically, a heaven, nor is it a tolerable part of the earth; but, in the heart of a soldier who faces death to preserve the liberty of his country, there is something that allies him clearly with the heaven of our thoughts.

We live in a world in which land grabbing has from the beginning been practiced. Primitive tribes fought for hunting grounds, nomadic peoples for pasturage, and agricultural ones for ample and permanent dwelling places. All these were exposed to attacks from intruders. Property in land and sovereignty over it were perpetual bones of contention, and each people was obliged to protect itself from spoilers.

Small states have nearly always been insecure. Powerful neighbors were forever seeking to absorb them, and not till comparatively recent times, when a quasi-guardianship was established over them, were these states measurably safe. The interest of a general community of states finally demanded that no one of the great ones should extend its area and its power by absorbing *ad libitum* the lesser domains upon its borders. Measures for preventing this were finally taken and for considerable periods the European community of states has had its way and the smaller members have been made materially safer than they had been. Nowhere have there been in modern times such great and lasting conquests as Romans and other ancient folk achieved. Rapacity, conquest, slavery, and then an empire enjoying internal peace under despotic rule — such was the sequence of events again and again in the ancient world.

Last and best known of these empires of antiquity was that of Rome, which prided itself on extending the *Pax Romana* over much of the known earth. For the annexed provinces the result was peace without liberty, but the fall of the empire meant a wild and perilous liberty with very little peace. Where the Caesars had ruled the war spirit was for centuries too rampant to permit the kind of state building that prepares the way for security. In time Europe began to take the shape with which we are now familiar — a community of states of widely different sizes, capable of coöperating for the promotion of their common interests and the protection of their liberties — though at times they have had to fight in order to do it. States repeatedly pooled forces of defense, and very enlightening is the record of their action for this purpose. It tells a tale from which the nations of today may profit.

Seldom or never does a modern state confess the act

of initiating a war; and this fact in itself attests the essential criminality of such action. It wrongs first the state that is attacked and secondly the international community. A population assailed usually awaits no formalities before defending itself, and, if there are other states so situated that their land or their freedom would be imperiled by the success of the aggression, they may be quick to make common cause with the defender. In this each state acts as guardian of its own rights; but the paramount interest in the case is international. The peace of the community must not be broken, and it rests with the community to see that it is not broken. To that end whenever a breach of the international peace occurs it must be able to see who has been guilty of breaking it. Each of the combatants will doubtless accuse the other of doing this, and if there were no possibility of testing such conflicting claims the effort to keep the peace by any common action of the nations would encounter a very serious obstacle. In order that the community should range its forces against aggression, it must be able clearly to distinguish it when it occurs. It must be a matter of common knowledge in advance of any breach of the peace, that international forces will oppose it. To the end that they may do so, they must be able to identify the assailants, and it must be known in advance that they can and will identify and resist them. Difficulties in the way of this achievement must, at all costs, be surmounted, and every covetous power must clearly see what resistance may be expected if it gives rein to its ambition. Not too early nor too clearly can the fact be established that a community of states, like a community of individuals, will know a breaker of the peace when they see him and be practically certain to curb his action. That will forestall and prevent the action. Potential defense is the only sufficient preventive of offense. The prospect of peace on our planet and of a life that is worth the living lies (1) in the fact that aggression is under moral and legal condemnation; (2) that it can be detected when it occurs; and (3) that it will surely encounter a resistance that is both righteous and effectual. If this means a peace that is ensured by a flaming sword, blessed be the flame that powers of evil will see and avoid; it will make the use of the blade unnecessary.

THE DEVIL'S DUE

THERE is no denying, and no need of denying, that man has accomplished important objects by fighting for them. His earliest and most desperate struggle was waged against other animals, and it ensured first his own survival and then his dominion over the animate world. This was sheer imperialism in its early form; the benefit resulting from it will not be challenged by the victors, and the vanquished are not in a position to present their case. It would be futile to claim that in contests with dumb animals man acted only on the defensive or that he was conscious of any ethical principle that forbade him to kill such creatures *ad libitum*. To this day the inherent rights of animals are very imperfectly recognized and still more imperfectly observed.

In the struggle for survival the hand that could grasp a club and the brain that could direct the manner of using it counted heavily in man's favor; but his social nature and the gift of speech counted for even more, since they enabled men to fight in armies, small or great. This was a preliminary stage of real warfare on our planet, where it has since raged so widely. In a true sense the substitution of organized war for desultory fighting was a forward step — the first step taken in the direction of international peace. It had the effect of substituting organized contention of masses of men for a mêlée of wild fighting by disorderly groups. It made hostilities intermittent instead of practically continuous.

Peace, as we have known it on our earth, has always existed at intervals only. Call forces together, meet the enemy, kill or be killed — such is the order for a time. Then follows a period, short or long, during which the belligerents allow each other to dwell unmolested. The organized struggles of men to possess and enjoy their heritage on the earth had as a first fruit the putting of time limits on deadly contentions. Wild tribes did not fight without ceasing — though they took to the warpath more frequently than did the small civilized ones. As the latter grew larger and became well established states, wars became still less frequent. In the jungle there had been no immunity from attacks, and among the early tribes such immunity was brief and uncertain. Between developed states there were longer and more assured respites from fighting; but only among advanced members of this class of states have peaceful intervals been long enough to allow arms to be laid aside in the happy consciousness of present safety. The dark feature of the outlook today is the possibility that the present interval of peace may end in the fiercest of wars. That possibility we still face; but, on the other hand, we can now for the first time entertain a reasonable hope that within the pale of civilization warfare will be generally suppressed.

A TENDER OF PEACE

By a natural action modern states have become fewer and greater than they were. Strong ones have absorbed weak neighbors, and this crude and simple type of imperialism has been a prominent feature of the modern world. In the ancient world this crude imperialism gave to conquered peoples one large offset for the loss of their independence; it kept them at peace with one another. Assyria, Persia, Egypt, Macedonia and Rome saved their subject peoples from fighting among themselves. On and beyond the boundaries of such empires fighting went on, but not, as a rule, within the boundaries, albeit the subject peoples were liable to be pressed into service, at need, for the foreign wars of the great empire. No peril ceaselessly impended over their hearths and homes, calling them ever and anon to the battlefield. So much the bloody warfare that created the empire afterwards did for its inhabitants. The old dangers returned when the great empire itself was disrupted. The greatest achievement of the modern world will consist in uniting for the first time permanent peace with liberty. The states of today are enjoying in very large measure each of these boons, and they can keep both — if they will.

Until a quite recent period conquests were made largely by means of superior weapons or tactics. If the best implements are everywhere to be had and if skill in using them is everywhere attainable, a state that is at war may be beaten if it cannot maintain its supply of such instruments unimpaired. Maintenance of equipment promises to be the special problem in future contentions. An elaborate enginery — guns, shells, tanks, aircraft, seacraft and the like — perishes rapidly in the using, and an ability to use it lavishly and still maintain the supply may decide a war. If most of the available men are needed in the battlefield, fighting machinery may have to be imported in great quantities; and if the foreign makers are disposed or pledged to send such supplies to one contestant and not to another, they can probably decide the issue of the war. If it is made known in advance of the outbreak of a war that arms and equipment will be furnished to one side and not to the other, the knowledge will go very far toward preventing the war altogether. If it is known (1) that the community of nations will unite to arm a defending state and not its assailant, (2) that the aggressive state will surely be identified, and (3) that it cannot expect supplies from the environing countries, while the defending state can get them in plenty — the assault may easily be prevented from occurring at all. There is a partial provision for a boycott of this kind in the compact of the League of Nations.

In order that this outcome may be assured, there must be an authoritative decision of the question which contestant is the aggressor, and which the defender. If that knowledge will surely be made public, it is only a supremely powerful state or a phenomenally foolish one that will persist in the attempt to crush and plunder another country. Potential defense is here at its best.

It will be possible to make widely known the fact that a decisive power will back any state that is wantonly assailed. It will be possible to ensure to it ample weapons and supplies and, so, to enable it to use its own man-power chiefly in the field. If that is done, there is small probability that an attack will be made at all unless the assailant is a giant or the victim a dwarf.

We shall see that the principle of potential defense has a very wide application and is the chief ground of hope for permanent peace at any time in the future. Any state or group of states that is able to decide the outcome of a threatened war can prevent the war if it is determined to do so. Conditional intervention by a superior force is the effective discourager of assaults. There will be no war in a world in which every power knows that if it enters on a marauding course of action it will encounter the forces of the community of states of which it is a member. Prudence will then reënforce conscience in bidding it keep the peace.

The foregoing pages describe conditions that will be recognized as real. They illustrate a law that has played a great part in history. Equal powers normally keep the peace with each other, but either of them may tender to a small power the kind of alternative with which our world is sadly familiar, " yield or be crushed." Unequal powers furnish a constant and tempting opportunity for wars of conquest. Rule out of consideration any scruples that might prevent a wanton seizure of land, rule out, also, the defensive leagues that lesser powers may otherwise form, and there remains a condition in which a natural tendency impels any strong state to grab the territory of a weaker one and so to make itself still stronger and better able to play the robber until the accessible territories are all under its sway. With moral forces lacking, with covetousness rampant, conquest and spoliation (the essential elements in the creating of empires) tend to continue until protective alliances put some check on this process.

POTENTIAL DEFENSE

WE have maintained that the prospect for peace in the world at large depends on something that is described by the two words in the title of this chapter. Actual defense is a part of actual war; but potential defense is a universal resource for preventing it, and we are pursuing no chimera when we depend on it for peace among nations. *It is a known power of defensive fighting that prevents offensive onsets.* A fortress at the mouth of a harbor cannot go abroad and attack foreign cities or fleets, but its power to repel attacks may prevent them from being made and thus may keep the peace. The more effectively its garrison can fight, the smaller is the probability of their having to fight. Any unconquerable agent of defense may do a perfect work without ever exercising its fighting power if only it stands obviously ready to use that power whenever aggressions occur.

Throughout the entire animate world a known fighting ability wards off attacks. The lion is above the danger of assault by other animals; at need he may become a terrible assailant, and this fact has its analogies. Unconquerable states are under a temptation to play a predatory rôle — with dire calamity for the victims. States that are too powerful to fear attacks may make them systematically — which means empire building. Power and an aggressive purpose mean war; a superior power that will shield the weak means peace.

The great states of the ancient world had no such natural coherence as that which the modern states have developed, and there was seldom any great and voluntary gathering of forces for common ends. As a rule a very powerful state could retain the dominion that its arms had secured for it until internal causes sapped its strength and made it easy to disrupt it. During its vigorous period the small countries within attacking distance of it lived in peril until they were conquered and absorbed by their powerful neighbor. When the empire fell contests between its divisions began again, and the strong gradually become stronger, as before, until in time a new empire developed.

Why is it that after the breaking up of the Western Roman Empire, some similar power did not replace it as had anciently been the rule? Beginnings in that direction were made, and Charlemagne gathered a great territory under his scepter; but his successors divided it, and it remained first for Genghis Khan and then for Tamerlane to play the Alexander. The shadow of some conquest hung over Europe until recently, when the hope began to be cherished that this danger might be averted and that states, great and small, might be able to live side by side without a renewal of empire building — and also without a need of devastating wars for the prevention of empire building. Within a few centuries the freedom of most countries in the western world has seemed to become measurably secure, but great wars have been required for making it so. Liberty and peace have not long been enjoyed together, but something has recently made that happy combination possible. It has prevented a repetition of the conquests of ancient times, and the nations now can, if they will, preserve their freedom without the actual bloodshed which was formerly necessary for that purpose. Centuries of medieval chaos following the fall of Rome ended in the building of a few great states and a multitude of small ones, among which the continent of Europe was divided. Wars innumerable resulted in this condition, which in itself invited a renewal of empire building. The mutual jealousy of large powers, however, gave a measure of protection to lesser ones, and the large states were cautious about fighting each other. Whenever neighboring countries are few, strong, and not very unequal, each is naturally reluctant to attack another or to allow any one of their number to attack a smaller one successfully. Wars became less constant than they had been. The group as a whole is now profoundly interested in preventing any one of its members from becoming great enough to build an empire after the ancient pattern.

There is a clear principle at the basis of the type of peace which has prevailed since the Thirty Years' War. It is a " bad gamble " for any two states of equal power to fight at all. The costs and losses of life that a war entails are so much deducted from the winnings of the victorious power, and they are crushing additions to the losses that the defeated one must accept. At a gaming table only a victim of " gamblers' insanity " would stake a large sum against a like amount if the chance of winning or losing were even, and if he had to pay a great fee for the privilege of making the play. Enormous has been the price of the privilege of making war. Winners and losers alike have had to pay cost bills, and, while the winner can at best only hope for a margin of gain over aggregate outlays, his victim must stagger under a crushing burden of outlays plus losses. Under a rule of reason (or anything that resembles it) equal states do not fight each other when for either of them defeat is about as probable as victory. In such a situation it may be said that a " balance of power " counts heavily as an influence for peace.

Through a period of about fifty years ending in 1864, five nations, all in one general class in point of strength, had possession of most of Europe, and it was then a truism that this fact was a prime influence in preventing war. What is not so generally known is that, at the opening of modern times, when a " balance of power " was consciously introduced as a feature of international relations, the term signified something quite different from this near-equality of forces. It expressed a noble and far-reaching purpose which nations on that continent have never abandoned. It afforded a forecast of the time when an entire community of independent states would stand ready to pool forces for thwarting dangerous aggressions. There is no doubt that for a certain time after 1648, when the Thirty Years' War ended, potential defense (that which, in case of need, is sure to be converted into active defense) counted decisively in preventing the grasps at wide dominion that would otherwise have occurred.

There was much in the Westphalian treaties of that date that foreshadowed the best elements in the international life of today. A dawning community consciousness expressed itself in provisions of these documents, and it has since ripened into concurrent action for promoting peace and general welfare. There were, even at that time, traces of the strong economic bonds that today make the world one organism — one living entity, in which each member exists and works not for itself alone but also for other members. Centuries ago division of labor and the exchanging of products were the order of the day, not only between different producers in the same country, but to a limited extent between those of different countries. Commerce has always created an international bond, and we shall find that the strength of it has now been raised to the nth power. A new type of interdependence has grown out of it and become the most conspicuous of all recent economic developments. The leading modern type of corporation has made itself, not only an incomparable producer, but in its way a world unifier.

The practical interdependence of nation and nation

POTENTIAL DEFENSE

is now the conspicuous fact. Germs of it appeared three centuries ago in the political world and have had a brilliant recent development. Organic union, economic and social, is the antithesis of war and the cause of unprecedented efforts to prevent it. It is a struggle by the genii of progress against old-time enemies. The practical world wants no more intentional and systematic rack and ruin. The code of ethics that once approved it is also among the discards of the present. We have reached a point in evolution in which righteousness and national interest call unitedly for permanent peace, and this will be had whenever it is known that if aggression occurs it will meet decisive resistance. The ensuring of such resistance is the chief task of our generation.

A TURNING POINT
IN HISTORY

BECAUSE of its length and the wild ravaging that attended it, the Thirty Years' War still holds the European record for destructiveness. If reports can be trusted it reduced the population of Germany to a third of its former number. In the later stages of the struggle combatants on both sides ravaged even their own lands when only that measure would prevent them from affording supplies for the enemy. At the beginning, the war aligned Protestants against Catholics; but the successes of the Emperor, Ferdinand the Second, put the liberty of many states in danger and so brought Catholic France into the field on the Protestant side. In the end all contestants became utterly war-weary and in the treaties of Westphalia they did their best to settle a great number of issues and especially to prevent the building of any dominant state by conquest and annexation.

In the entire situation there was not a little that foreshadowed the conditions of 1919. Three decades of rack and ruin had furnished an irresistible incentive for trying to avert a repetition of this calamity. The world knows by recent experience that a Sheol seen in all its terrors is a powerful anti-Sheol influence, and in

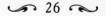

40733

A TURNING POINT

1648, emerging from the pit that had engulfed them and with its horrors freshly in mind, the people of Europe were united by a bond of common and vital interest in preventing a recurrence of the strife. Over the vast cemetery of much of the continent, nations clasped hands in a united effort to curb imperialism, which was the chief source of danger.

For lack of a workable plan for uniting in one league a miscellany of states of every size and kind, Protestant Sweden and Catholic France were commissioned to act for the powers represented in the treaty in opposing any grasp at wide dominion. Under this arrangement any nation that should enter on a career of conquest would face in addition to its intended victims those two great powers and others that might join them in opposing the aggressive attempt. This dual commission never actually used its joint authority, and it was not very many years before France herself under Louis the Fourteenth embarked on a course of conquest such as the commission was enjoined to prevent. It would be a rash inference, however, that would conclude from these facts that the dual commission for preserving the general freedom was without important influence. For a time it afforded a potential defense against attacks on the lesser states, and later it was a temporary barrier against dangerous growth by larger ones.

In 1648 the so-called "balance of power" was brilliantly advocated and generally accepted as a means of blocking ambitious schemes of imperial conquest.

A TENDER OF PEACE

At the present time, the conception of the goal to be sought is broader. And although the principle of international action remains valid, the methods need to be brought within the orderly procedures of international law. Such orderly procedures must now be substituted for the arbitrary action of states of the older monarchic type.

POLITICAL EVOLUTION

IN an important way war is practical economics reversed. Its action undoes quickly and thoroughly much of what labor and capital have done. It leaves broken walls and stone heaps where dwellings, shops, schoolhouses, libraries, and churches formerly stood. It turns to tragic use the command over great forces of nature which industry has suddenly acquired and destroys much of the fruit which this harnessing of power has already yielded. Can the cause of the blight be removed, and can it be removed quickly enough to prevent another Armageddon? If it were depravity in individuals of our race that caused this savagery it would already be so firmly fastened on us that working for permanent peace would be chasing a rainbow; the coming of peace would have to wait for a moral millennium. The saving fact is that wars are not caused by the personal depravity of all the members of a population. Any civilized people today is far above the moral level at which it would be capable of willfully inaugurating a carnival of bloodshed. There is a sociological principle that sometimes causes a body of intelligent men to act as one composite fool, and the same principle may cause a great mass of good men to take on the guise of collective depravity. Kind-hearted citizens in a united mass are capable of temporarily playing the savage maniac, and they may adopt policies that attest this fact. They may then so act as practically to turn some part of the world into a shambles. If the super-Armageddon comes at all, it will be because what purports to be a superior race of men persists in ideas and practices inherited from savages. The conditions that rulers and ruled are now facing are unlike those that were confronted even by their recent ancestors, and they are utterly unlike those of more remote ancestors, except in a latent capacity for collective murder.

Our practical world is in essential respects a new one. It has undergone a quick transformation of its entire economic system, and its political system has felt the effects of this. Big business is dominant in world economics; democracy is dominant in politics; and the two contrasted facts, taken together, can be interpreted as full of promise for the near future. A combination of seemingly opposite tendencies, each of which considered separately is disquieting, may together remand to the past all procedure that involves systematic destruction.

No argument is needed for proving that a radical change in the business of the world has occurred within the easy recollection of elderly men. Industrial machinery is now the ruling power of a wider realm than it ever before ruled — and the end is not yet. Until lately, moreover, we had a national production with international exchanges. We studied the wealth of nations as affected by their relations to one another, and the resulting system is now becoming, at bottom, a world economy. The whole of it reacts on the several parts and shapes them more and more, until each country becomes largely what the world has made it. Markets encircle the globe, not merely because goods can now be quickly and cheaply carried from land to land, although this fact counts as a powerful influence, and not merely because selling agencies can be established almost anywhere, though this fact also has its importance. The great corporation that is today typical of the producers of most commodities can itself be domiciled in many lands. " Ubi bene ibi patria " is its serious rule of action.

The holding company — a somewhat disquieting feature of present-day business — is tying different lands together in a way that is transforming their conditions, largely for the better. Fortunately the present essay undertakes to discuss only one feature of this radical change, namely, how does it affect the prospect of peace? The answer is that it distinctly favors it. With nearly every great consolidated business establishing branch corporations in a number of leading countries, there is already at work a unifying influence extending throughout the world. This means a closer and closer interdependence of the different lands on one another, and it will involve in each land a personal mingling of the men whose interests unite them in an anti-war policy. Their clienteles, extending throughout the world, are practically at one in calling for peace.

A TENDER OF PEACE

The " financial world " includes the men who either own or are maintained by it and are hostages for peaceful policies by their several governments. They are well trained in the practical art of working in a common cause. In this instance self-interest and high morality are in accord.

World economics demand the prevention of war. Wherever the shadow of this blight darkens the horizon, self-interest and ethics unitedly require that the nations shall bar it from the earth. A widespread peril calls for the quick training of a civilian force capable of averting it. Populations eager for peace are becoming more and more able to unite in taking measures that ensure it, and the practical world is becoming a natural peace society. This fact applies with emphasis to organized labor as well as to massed capital. Both demand peace in order that life may be worth living — *and yet war at its worst is a terrible possibility.*

In maintaining that big business makes for peace we are not demanding that the world should be made safe for actual plutocracy. In opposition to war, massed capital and massed labor are as one. Antedating the international aims of capital were those of organized labor — at first for good wages, indeed, but later for the peace by which that end and other ends can be attained. Financial problems often lead to international disagreements; but these are, as a rule, highly " justiciable," and a special court can be trusted to deal with them. As a conspicuous result of recent wars some old-time despotisms are at an end. The world has become generally safe for democracy; and by reason of democracy, it has been made more nearly safe from war than it has ever been before. Industrial populations have overwhelming motives for demanding peace.

Without maintaining that among modern republics the coveting of neighboring land is extinct, it may be said with confidence that it has become perilous to foster it, and that nowhere in the world can it now assert itself without at once meeting effective condemnation. The condition of the world in which we now live demands that nations shall not despoil each other. Their dealings, like those of individuals, must recognize a reign of law, which involves precepts with force behind them. It means a new and effectve mode of accomplishing what the " balance of power " made a rude early effort to accomplish, namely, the putting of the power of a community of nations behind any of their number that may be assailed in violation of pledges taken by them all.

ENTANGLING
ALLIANCES

THERE is a wealth of argument in the two words at the head of this chapter. Americans have dreaded and avoided " entanglements," and an appeal to the fear of them has helped to keep our country out of the League of Nations. In an earlier day, when only the Atlantic border of their continent was tenanted by Europeans, the colonies united in a long and desolating war in order to disentangle themselves — first, from particular meshes that the British government was throwing about them, and, later, from subjection to that government itself. " In the course of human events " it had " become necessary to dissolve " a political bond and to " assume among the nations of the earth a separate and equal station."

In the war that followed this action the federated colonies formed an alliance with France and received from that country invaluable aid. Money, supplies, ships, and military forces came to them from their ally at a critical time and helped to decide the issue of the struggle. The outcome was the freedom and equality called for by the Declaration of Independence. The alliance that accomplished this was highly " disentangling," in that it helped our country to cast off a hampering tie with England and to enter a brilliant course of independent growth.

Treaties impose obligations on all the states that sign them, and treaties which were executed between France and America during the American Revolution provided that if as a result of these compacts England should declare war on France, our country would make common cause with its new ally in resisting. Here was a possible entanglement of another kind; but the British government found it prudent to refrain from such a declaration of war, and the obligation for joint resistance lapsed. In 1792, when France was engaged in a European war, Washington and his cabinet decided that our country was not under obligation to take part in it. A defensive war against England was designated in the treaty, while the war that the French were at this later date waging was considered offensive. It had, moreover, been brought on by a revolutionary government with which the Americans had made no contract. The Americans were genuinely grateful to the French as a people, and if England had then attacked France they might have responded heartily to the call of their former ally for aid. It is a happy circumstance that in the late war our gratitude to France expressed itself practically and generously. Very appropriately did an American general say as he landed on French soil with the first quota of American troops, "Lafayette, we are here."

This bit of familiar history illustrates the type of

entanglement that our people dread. They have no liking for obligations that may send American boys across the sea to take part in wars in which our own rights are not assailed. In 1800 the first platform of the Democratic Party (then called " Republican ") contained a paragraph declaring its " opposition to linking ourselves, by new treaties, with the quarrels of Europe." This means that in all that pertains to war and peace continental boundaries have great significance; but alliances that cross these lines may be made to count heavily in favor of peace. If the world at any time reaches a status of complete exemption from warfare, it will be because one continent has first reached that status and other continents have followed suit. The great boon will doubtless come not first to the world and then to continental divisions of it but first to a single continent, then to other continents, and finally to all. Very far, however, is this from meaning that the purpose ultimately to banish war should not be world-wide from the start. A peaceful earth has from the beginning been the ultimate aim, and the time has now arrived for shaping policies having that fact in direct view.

Treaties may liberate, not merely entangle; and the League which many nations have made, and which all are invited to join, is distinctly liberating in its result for the signers. Defensive unions formed by states which if separate would have been in danger of subjugation are preservers of liberty and preventers of what may be treated as the most complete form of entanglement — the absorption of weak states by conquest. A contract by a number of states to fight jointly in defense of any one of the signers that may be attacked, should from the first reduce the amount of fighting that is done. Such contracts have actually gone far toward preventing conquest and domination. Limited defensive alliances have contributed much to the peace of the world and very much to its liberty. They have bought these boons at a cost that is contingent only and the number of wars which have been prevented is much larger than the number in which the contracting parties have been obliged to engage.

Throughout the centuries intervening between the Westphalian treaties and the World War, coöperative defense has been part of the prevailing order of national action. Conflicts occurring in spite of this *régime* were often costly, but the number was reduced and the freedom of the allied countries was generally preserved. A check was put on powers that cherished imperial ambitions. Free states, therefore, by pooling forces and actually repelling a common enemy, may prevent a series of wars that otherwise would have occurred.

There is always danger that one great alliance may, in its entirety, be drawn into a war with a similar one; witness the greatest and most recent of such struggles — the World War. These and other sinister possibilities formerly impended over a field within which there was no general defensive compact. Before the advent of a general League, it was local combinations for defense that constituted the best that the world was able to offer for safeguarding peace and freedom. If there is any faith to be put in the teachings of recent history and in the daily record of current events, the League of Nations is an incomparably better resource than such alliances. If it should disband, even reluctant America would be shocked by the perils to which much of the world would at once be exposed. The League is a protective rampart even for the country that has held aloof from membership in it; disbanding it would throw its present members on the very doubtful resource of local combinations for defense, and the danger of a general struggle would be imminent.

For three centuries Europe has been an active storm center from which America has been comparatively remote. Our statesmen have protested against a defensive union of our country with any single foreign country. The seas have discouraged other powers from attacking us. A microscopic army long sufficed for our needs, as did our little wooden navy. That attitude can no longer be held, for a great war, if it should occur, might enmesh us as did the recent one. If so, could our fighting power at once shield us from disaster? Would a good policy now require us to raise our army and navy to the nth degree? We can do better than that, and far better than we have done in all that concerns the war and peace of the future. A reversal of this lone-hand policy is obviously the safer one. The existence of a league of nations having America among its members might, in 1914, have prevented the war that drew in America as one of the contestants.

The teachings of the immediate past call with unparalleled emphasis for a concurrent action by Europe and America that will ensure to both continents a brighter prospect of peaceful living than either of them has ever enjoyed. If in foreign lands wars were predestined to occur, anything that would draw our country into such wars would be very much to be dreaded; but it is complete prevention of such warfare that is now in view, and the line of action that bids fair to secure it has not been initiated and has scarcely been discussed. In order that peace may be made secure, America must lend the strongest support that she is capable of lending to the anti-war institutions of the world. These are in an incipient stage and need developing in order to make peace secure on any continent.

There is as little doubt as there is about any fact of the future that the older world has recently created institutions for rendering to the entire human race a supreme service, and America should welcome a share in it. Our country should join the procession and not tardily follow it. A few truths, axioms of the peace problem, are enough to indicate the right course for all countries to pursue. Potential resistance to aggression is the ordained peace-preserving force. When it is universally known that defenders stand ready and able

to defeat aggression, aggression will not occur. The way
is clear for making this assurance good on both sides
of the Atlantic, and America must not fail to have a
part in it. Whatever she can do for this purpose out-
side of the League, she can do within it many times
better. An all-important fact today is that lasting peace
can be maintained in the storm center of the world —
the European continent. The fate of all nations on our
planet depends in a high degree on what is done in that
central field.

DETECTING
AGGRESSION

AS we have seen, the outlook for future peace depends on the success of the nations in forestalling and preventing aggressive action; and this, in turn, depends on their power to detect aggression in its initial stage. Many nations are now leagued for these purposes; and if by acting concurrently they succeed in accomplishing them, humanity will have entered a happier realm than it has ever before seen except in visions.

As we have said, the power to defeat an assailant would be futile, possibly even pernicious, if there were no sure rule for promptly identifying the assault when it occurs. The nations must know at once when one of their number has done something that by an accepted test is accounted as an attack. The getting of positive proof of such an offense may encounter difficulties, and unless these can be surmounted the entire effort to prevent war will labor under a perilous disability. Mistaken judgment on this point might cause the community of nations to range its united forces against an innocent defender, and inability to form any clear judgment would paralyze its effort to keep the peace in any way.

The most impressive fact in this connection is that a particular rule which has been suggested and widely supported for locating the responsibility for a war, would, if practically applied, be likely to condemn the actual defender. This rule would pronounce guilty any state that, " having pledged itself to allow its quarrels with other states to be arbitrated or adjudicated, actually resorts to war for settling them." Let us see how, in certain contingencies, this rule might work.

I. If in any case both contestants have signed the pledge and both afterwards fight, the proposed test affords in itself alone no basis for decision whatever. If the actual culprit is convicted, it must be on other grounds.

II. If neither contestant has made such a pledge and both fight over their dispute, nothing has been done by either of them that under the proposed rule alone would constitute aggression.

III. If one contestant has signed the peace-and-arbitration compact and the other has not done so, various decisions are possible; but that which would merely condemn the party that had taken the pledge and was afterwards found fighting, might condemn the actual defender in the case and exonerate the assailant. What if the state that is under the pledge loyally keeps it until the guns of the enemy are throwing shells into its border towns and then replies in kind? Very obviously it is the defender, but the proposed rule, if literally applied, would brand it as the culprit, range the League of Nations against it, and mark it for boycott and the other measures to which the League may resort for crushing aggression.

DETECTING AGGRESSION

The rule as commonly stated is glaringly incomplete. If we proceed to complete it, we shall find that the new element which we must introduce is, at bottom, the complete rule that is needed, and if practically applied would by itself alone distinguish the guilty party against whom the forces of the community of states should be ranged. What the promise to abstain from warfare may well accomplish is to make an aggression more guilty than it would otherwise have been. It would especially invite the fellow signers of the peace pact to rally behind the nation so assailed. The fact of a broken pledge is not the essence of the aggressive act; but it makes the act conspicuous and doubly guilty.

A rule that suffices for identifying an aggressor is entirely compatible with one that gauges the degree of iniquity of his action. It is of the utmost importance that the severe verdict should never be visited on any country that is forced to fight and does so righteously and heroically. It is to such a state that the associated nations in such a league intend to lend support. They can well afford to spend any sum of money and any amount of effort in making certain which of two con-contestants is actually guilty in any war that may occur. In the entire effort of the present-day world to keep the peace it is indispensable that it should be able to make certain, in every instance in which the peace has been broken, who did the deed — who ended the peaceful status, created a state of war, and so made resistance necessary. It is here maintained that this momentous question can be satisfactorily answered by a general community of states if they will make use of the power of united action that recent compacts and inherent justice have given to them. A league of nations is indispensable for success in this supreme achievement. The world, as it stands today, is able to supply the essential element that is as yet absent from its program of action.

A precedent for barring active armies from a well-defined zone was created by the treaty of Versailles, which for a time excluded them from a broad area extending eastward from the Rhine and the Belgian border. In one of the Locarno treaties there was a provision that involved such a zone, and the need for it seems to be recognized in both the provisions of the Geneva Protocol and the compact of the League of Nations. If certain areas can be closed against all armies, fighting can be halted until the motive for it has been removed. An all-important rôle in the repression of warfare seems destined to be played by such a provision.

The joint authority of many nations may now be invoked to create barriers against assault whenever it may seem to be pending. Unfriendly armies equipped for fighting must be kept at a distance from each other much as two armed and angry men may be kept apart by policemen. We are nearing a field of discussion in which technical knowledge of warfare and experience in it are helpful in revealing effective methods of keeping the states out of it. New defensive plans need to be made, new orders must be enforced, and difficulties that are created by time-honored practice must be overcome. The war demon has artifices, and one of them is putting obstacles in the way of convicting the state that begins a war and then accuses its victim of beginning it. That must be prevented once for all; and it will be so if there is any virtue in present statesmanship.

A demilitarized zone on each side of the common boundary of two states that are drifting into war may be so watched as to make it impossible to conceal or disguise any large body of troops within it. In the laws and the prevailing practices of nations, neutral states are *ipso facto* demilitarized in so far as the movements of mutually hostile forces are concerned. These forces must not cross such territory. The plan here suggested is to put on a similar footing a zone on each side of the boundary line of any two contiguous countries, and to see to it that the excluding orders are recognized. What these measures should accomplish is to make it impossible for a great body of hostile troops to reach the territory of its victims without letting the knowledge of this intention promptly reach the rest of the world. There must be no stealing a march on an unprepared nation. If no unfriendly force can enter the border area without detection, if such a hostile action, when made at all, must be made under the eyes of all men, a very modicum of reason will deter any power from making it unless the power is strong enough to defy much of the world.

A TENDER OF PEACE

Certain it is that aggressions must at all costs be halted if the nations expect to stay out of the pit from which they have recently emerged. A full discussion of the procedure required for this purpose would be beyond the scope of this volume. Practical questions concerning it multiply when one takes into account the capabilities of aircraft and seacraft. Conceivably an aerial squadron might, by aid of clouds, cross almost any zone without being seen, but hardly without being in some way detected, unless the mechanism of such craft is radically changed. A great squadron bent on bombing cities would certainly not escape detection, and its murderous purpose would be an irresistible plea for the measure that the Covenant of the League of Nations is actually pledged to take — namely, to treat an overt attack on any of its members as an attack on the League in its entirety. This declaration should reduce the probability of the attack almost to nil.

Patrolling the peace belt in times of danger will have to be done by a commission representing the League and acting in accordance with established rules. It goes without saying that in a crisis no waiting to adopt rules should be needed or tolerated. In the present peaceful time there should be no serious difficulty in formulating an adequate code. The League of Nations exists and can create whatever commissions the adoption of a plan of action may require. Beyond the scope of this small volume are discussions of detailed modes of procedure. Well within every man's sphere of thought and action

DETECTING AGGRESSION

is the question, " Can aggressions be identified, exposed, and effectively resisted? " The answer is an assured " *Yes*."

" In time of peace prepare for war " has meant "train and arm the forces that will be needed when war comes "; but it is capable of meaning " prepare to avert war." Perfect the League of Nations for that purpose or, at all events, make sure that an agency exists which will know when the peace has been broken and who broke it. Anything that will accomplish this will be in harmony with the deepest wishes of the human race. The proposed method will apply on an international scale an expedient that has always been effective in maintaining peace within single nations. This expedient is capable of maintaining peace within an international community. It should make aggressive action between states always discoverable. The offender must betray himself, and the interstate community must do the rest, including the putting of the combined forces of the international community behind the victim of the assault. This assured outcome of a common defense can be trusted to prevent offense and ensure peace, which means that the assurance of a common defense of each peaceful nation is the condition on which peace is now tendered to the continent on which from the Middle Ages to the present day warfare has been a supreme and ever-impending scourge. It should prevent war in Europe.

WAR AND DEMOCRACY

A WAR of conquest and empire building may end by establishing peace throughout a large area. A victorious monarch has reason for preventing further hostilities within the area of his conquests. Napoleon might thus have pacified Europe if conquering all of it had been within the scope of what he called his " destiny." Supremely fortunate will be the world at large and Europe in particular if the peace which might have followed such a general surrender of freedom shall now be attained and preserved without so great a sacrifice. This will be accomplished if the time comes when an assault on any one member of an unconquerable League will be identified and resisted by all the others. This status has been approached in Europe but has not been actually reached there or elsewhere. Forces of civilization may still be used in struggles that are very decivilizing. For averting this calamity, it may be indispensable to pool defensive forces on a scale that will surpass any similar action heretofore taken.

The Europe of today needs above all else a union for ending interstate warfare within its area. It should unite all states on that continent under provisions that will make the combination as a whole unconquerable. The League of Nations now existing has made an inspiring approach to this goal. As a defensive union it is probably stronger than any other thus far formed, and it may become so effective and so permanent that it will rule interstate assaults definitively from the central division of the earth. Its existence means a tender of peace, first to this geographical division, and later to others. If it will adopt an effective plan of action — one which each state in its membership will follow whenever a war is initiated within the boundaries of the European continent — aggressions there will without doubt cease to occur. Peace in Europe will then be lasting, but it will have required new and effective measures to make it so.

The problem of peace will be solved, if it is solved at all, by an assured pooling of forces of defense which neither present nor future Caesars will dare to challenge. A defensive power which is continent-wide, and which will become active at need, will do for nations which it guards what effective policing does for all the wards of a city. It will repress lawlessness within the great commonwealth in which nations, in their entirety, are the units.

It follows that the problem of peace is the problem of shaping and adopting a plan of concurrent defensive action that will be followed by nations when the peace of their continental domain is threatened.

There have been times in the history of various nations when private citizens have been armed and called into the field in defense of public order. The fact that in any nation they can be so summoned gives a latent power to the police corps, and nearly always removes the need of actually calling private citizens into the field. The divisions of Europe may keep order among themselves by methods somewhat akin to those used by citizens in a well-regulated city — without the necessity of actually fighting for it.

The contrast between the Europe that the world has known and the one that it will know if a reign of peace is there established, is radical; but the mode of ensuring that outcome is simple. It would be capable of doing for a great part of the inhabited earth what has a myriad of times been accomplished for particular sections. Europe is clearly invited to recognize the principle on which lasting peace within small areas is regularly maintained and to apply it throughout its grand domain.

Governing any free part of our world means asserting the dominant will of a majority of its inhabitants. A particular type of government may be opposed and sometimes displaced; but that invariably means that another type has supporters who hope to establish it. Opposition to government as such has no support. Rebels, if successful, appoint rulers of their own choosing; *and rule as such is rarely lacking.*

What is necessary for peace in Europe is the application within a great body of states of the principle that is recognized within each separate one of them. In a highly important way the democratic principle is applied when these states form a league for any com-

mon purpose. The greatest of purposes (verily a supreme end in the view of the people of Europe) should
be and is a union of states in the form of *an interstate
democracy — a political body within which each state
in its entirety is, as it were, one citizen.* When this greater
democracy rules, peace will probably come to stay forever.

How must Europe as a whole enforce peace among
its continental divisions? Shall it base its action on the
expressed will of a majority of the states? If so, in
what way shall this will make itself known? Evidently
any prohibition of aggression must have force behind
it in order to be effective. We may note aspects of the
present condition of European states that give promise
of success in thus keeping the peace. In every free
state, great or small, the loyal inhabitants stand ready
to unite if necessary against rebellion. If the members
of a strong union of states are as ready to act together
in cases of need, uprisings will not occur; no single
state will rebel.

One cardinal conclusion is happily beyond dispute —
namely, that states as members of a greater community
can ensure peace by a general anti-war pledge with
adequate force behind it. Any marauding state must
be halted and coerced into peaceful action. There must
be no aggression, no crossing of boundaries under arms
and with hostile intention.

When an army is mobilizing and is evidently prepar-
ing to assail another, it will be incumbent on the peace-

ful states on the same continent to halt this movement. If the order to halt is reënforced by the massing of a superior army, there will be little danger that the order will be disregarded. A wholesome respect for the will and the power of a continental union of states should suffice to avert assaults on any country in this area. Very transforming in its effects should be the compact that in clear terms will call armies of Europe into the field to halt an invasion of territory on that continent.

Is not this intervention actual warfare — something which we aim to prevent? It is the type of fighting in which a single shot may prevent a hundred shots that would otherwise have been fired. Policemen's clubs and guns are supremely peaceful instruments — albeit they are sometimes used with a disabling effect on would-be breakers of the law. The entire international peace movement depends for success on the power of the guardians of public peace and safety to use weapons when assaults cannot otherwise be halted. This type of public service, indispensable as it is for maintaining any government, may also be rendered to an international entity — the great community of which states are members. Given aggressive purposes and no adequate means of defeating them, the greatest of crimes and misdemeanors will prevail unhindered. The safety and happiness of nations depends upon their power *to avert this calamity by their joint action.*

CONCLUSION

" LET us have peace," as said General Grant. A highway leading out of the region of wars is now open, and the nations, one and all, have a vital interest in following it. If a time comes when an assault by one state against another will without fail enlist an unconquerable force on the defender's side, the problem of preventing warfare will be solved and peace will rule as never before on the earth. Without a prospect of such intervention there is no assurance that wars will not ever and anon recur — unless the last war creates a new all-embracing empire.

The international sky now abounds in storm clouds — and albeit they may be more distant than those of an earlier time, they are also much darker. Pledges of peaceful behavior may not of themselves prevent war. When all the states on a continent are definitely enlisted in a protective union and are taking practical measures for preventing aggression which would result in war, there will be a stronger assurance of peace throughout that quarter of the world than has ever before been attained. These facts plainly call for a supreme achievement by nations of our time. They can now grasp a boon that has never before been within grasping distance.

The nations can convert uncertain hopes into realities. They can put an end to a scourge that is now as old as the dominion of man on our planet. Deadly conflicts in Europe can certainly be prevented if the governments on that continent will unitedly so ordain. A state can if it so chooses play the bully; what is needed in Europe is a union of powers which can and will deal effectively with bullying. It must halt hostilities if they occur but must aim to prevent them from occurring.

The law-abiding nations, one and all, can if they so will stand ready to defend with united forces any member of their group that may be attacked. Such action was clearly in the minds of the statesmen who formed the League of Nations, members of which are required by their present code to " boycott " the state that is assaulting another. Although in a long war a boycott would not fail to weigh very heavily against the assailant, it is less effectual in short and decisive attacks. For the latter, there is imperative need of a power of intervention and a known purpose to use it when necessary.

A strong protecting union is the obvious *sine qua non* of effective action for preventing warfare. The compact of the League of Nations requires its signers to put themselves unitedly on the side of any of their number that may be attacked; but their prescribed action (the boycotting of assailants) may of itself fall short of what is needed. Further measures will then be necessary. Quite decisive must be the action of the International

CONCLUSION

Council in any critical exigency. The defeat of invaders and the winning of safety for intended victims must be fully assured.

There is a general impression that in Europe conquering ambitions are not extinct albeit they are checked by a respect for what the nations on that continent may unitedly do if an old-time conquest is undertaken. The fear of what they probably would do, if a grabbing of territory should occur, is the principal deterrent that now prevents it from occurring. Clearly needed is a stronger influence of this kind. Aggression must be made to face failure, and the nations must make this outcome practically a certainty. On this condition only is peace today tendered to the central division of the world.

Very far on the highway toward universal peace will the entire world have advanced when Europe stands ready to use its available power in defeating assaults that may be made within its area. When the states on that continent are ready to make common cause in repelling attacks, attacks will not be made. Since all the states would then be virtually assailed when any one of them is literally so, their united forces would be available for resistance.

We are here in a region of study on which history throws light. The world must not wait for the expected catastrophe to occur before making ready for it. A plan for effectual defense may if generally accepted prevent the armed assault altogether. The present peaceful interval affords a golden opportunity for uniting Europe in a defensive alliance that no single state and no limited group of states will ever venture to assail.

The practical art of warfare makes progress even in intervals of peace, and a defensive union should keep pace with it. States that are members of the League will have in this respect a decided advantage over any that hold aloof from it. One and all, they can be free, democratic, peaceful, and secure.

The art of common defense acquired by a group of countries should make them in truth a " family of nations " as we are wont to call them. That same defensive art should open the gateways through which the states of the world must go before the final portal is reached and they enter the realm of unbroken peace — the goal of humanity during its weary journey. International aggressions may then become so perilous for the assailant that they will not again occur. A workable plan for common defense by the countries of Europe is the natural reliance for keeping peace on that continent. Strong and ambitious nations can be trusted to leave weak neighbors undisturbed if an attack in force on any one of them will at once call out the protecting armies of the others.

" The next war," which the world now rightly dreads, may, if it occurs at all, be reduced to a grasp at territory, a resistance by the dwellers thereon, then a quick expulsion of the invaders by intervening powers. If no protective union is established and if a *laisser faire*

CONCLUSION

policy is generally accepted, the next war may be the renewal of successful empire building. If the World War has had the effect of making all Europeans dread and seek to prevent another one, it has put civilized life on a level never before reached.

From what fate can defensive coöperation henceforth save the world? Will it prevent warfare as former years have known it? It will do vastly more than that. The life-destroying arts have a brilliant list of mechanical and chemical achievements. Aircraft can now supplement seacraft, with one result that is ominous indeed. It adds the sky to the land and the sea, as an arena for murderous action. Poisonous gases are the natural and most effective of instruments available for use by ships of the air, and crowded cities are most easily available for their attacks. Women and children are necessarily the chief victims. An unparalleled massacre of noncombatants awaits the advent of the next war in which aircraft will figure. Given gaseous poisons with airships for carrying them, as a leading feature of future wars, the nations must banish the war demon or be victims of the most savage of his assaults. We have here reached the stage to which the peace following the World War has carried the community of European states. This stage, with all its ominous features, yet represents potentially a change for the better. The world has a brilliant goal in sight, and the route to it is clear.

COLUMBIA UNIVERSITY PRESS
Columbia University
New York

———

FOREIGN AGENT
OXFORD UNIVERSITY PRESS
Humphrey Milford
Amen House, London, E. C. 4